1 MONTH OF
FREE
READING

at
www.ForgottenBooks.com

By purchasing this book you are eligible for one month membership to ForgottenBooks.com, giving you unlimited access to our entire collection of over 1,000,000 titles via our web site and mobile apps.

To claim your free month visit: www.forgottenbooks.com/free895211

ISBN 978-0-265-82652-2
PIBN 10895211

UNITED STATES DEPARTMENT OF AGRICULTURE
PRODUCTION AND MARKETING ADMINISTRATION
INFORMATION SERVICE
150 Broadway
New York 7, New York

Y O U R   F A M I L Y ' S   F O O D

For the Week of March 3, 1947

(Topics of the Week:
  Cheese Grading
  Eggs plentiful
  Sugar Notes
  Plentifuls

ANNOUNCER: Here is YOUR FAMILY'S FOOD...a program designed to keep
             you informed on factors affecting your daily food, and
             brought to you by Station _____ in cooperation with
             the United States Department of Agriculture. Our studio
             guest today is _____ _____, representing the
             Production and Marketing Administration office in
             _____. What's the topic for today, _____?

PMA: Hello, _____. I've got several things to talk
             about today. First a little something about cheese...
             then some information on eggs...and a word or two about
             sugar.

ANNOUNCER: That's quite a mixture. Of course, you've got the
             start of a cheese omelet there...but I don't know just
             where the sugar would fit in.

PMA: Oh, we'll find a place for it, _____.

ANNOUNCER: That brings up the subject of cheese...anything special
             happening?

PMA: Nothing spectacular. It's just that we Americans are eating more cheese than ever before...the Bureau of Agricultural Economics says we averaged 7 pounds per person last year. For the 20 years before the war, the yearly average was about $4\frac{1}{2}$ pounds.

ANNOUNCER: I guess lots cf people acquired a taste for cheese during the war, when they used it in place of other things.

PMA: Undoubtedly that had quite a bit to do with it. Consumption figures during the past three or four years show that as soon as civilians could get plenty of cheese after the war, they really dug in.

ANNOUNCER: What kind of cheese do people prefer --- American?

PMA: Now you're getting involved. But since folks are taking such an interest in cheese, perhaps we can tell them a little something about it.

ANNOUNCER: You can tell me exactly what is meant by "process" cheese, as a starter.

PMA: You're getting ahead of me. I haven't answered your previous question yet...which referred to the type of cheese preferred. Figures show that of the 7 pounds we ate last year, more than $4\frac{1}{2}$ pounds was American cheddar...with the remainder divided among all other varieties. Now, to answer your question about "process" cheese...the familiar loaf cheese is the

PMA:
(continued)
more common process type, but it's cheddar just the same. The "process" consists of testing, blending, and combining cheddar from different cures, pasteurizing the lot, and packing it. Thus you're sure of buying a cheese that always tastes the same.

ANNOUNCER: Oh, well then all of the trade varieties of cheese --- you know, the cheese spreads and the small packages --- are made the same way I suppose?

PMA: Yes, most of them are simply different blends of cheddar, with varying amounts of moisture for ease in spreading. The more moisture, the easier cheese spreads. At the same time, though, soft cheese doesn't keep as well as the dryer, hard cheese.

ANNOUNCER: Say, I'm learning things fast today. But what about the American-made foreign cheese? Stuff like American Swiss, or Blue cheese.

PMA: Now, of course, you're getting away from Cheddar. American Swiss is made about like the original Swiss. Many kinds of cheese are named for the places they were first produced, and we continue to use those names. You mentioned Blue cheese...that's simply American roquefort. I'm afraid the exact curing methods for different varieties are a little too deep for me.

ANNOUNCER: I don't wonder...cheese-making is a craft, I guess. Anyway, I understand it's highly technical in this country. And in Europe, of course, the art of making

ANNOUNCER: Cheese is handed down from generation to generation. But
(continued)
           I do have one question. What are the holes in Swiss

           cheese for?

PMA: You know, _____, when I decided to talk a little

           bit about cheese today, I just knew someone would ask

           that...so I prepared myself.

ANNOUNCER: If you have the straight answer, I'd sure welcome it.

PMA: Well. despite all the old jokes about the holes in Swiss

           cheese, the fact is that unless they _were_ there, you

           wouldn't _have_ Swiss cheese --- foreign or domestic. The

           holes --- which are called "eyes" in cheese circles ---

           are made by the escaping gases during the curing process.

ANNOUNCER: That's the second time you've referred to "curing". May-

           be you'd better explain the word.

PMA: Well, curing is done by storing the cheese at the proper

           temperature, to allow the acids or various organisms to

           do their work. It's also called "ripening".

ANNOUNCER: Then the common cottage cheese that we make at home is

           unripened...?

PMA: That's exactly right...and a good example, too. Cottage

           cheese comes, as we know, from sour milk. Then we have

           cream cheese, and this is made from sour _cream_. Now, if

           you go a step further, as the French did, and _ripen_

           cream cheese under proper conditions, you have Neufchatel

           ((NUF-SHA-TEL)) cheese. However, _domestic_ Neufchatel,

PMA:
(continued)   I'd better add, is not cured, being made from various grades of milk running from cream to skim.

ANNOUNCER: I suppose the differences in types of cheese --- their flavor, at least --- result from the richness of the milk, and the curing or ripening

PMA: You're learning fast. Actually, there are only about 20 varieties, although there are at least 400 names for cheese.

ANNOUNCER: Can cheese be graded?

PMA: It certainly can..and is. The Dairy and Poultry Branch of the Department of Agriculture maintains a cheese grading service, available to any plant that wants it and is willing to pay for it.

ANNOUNCER: But likes and dislikes in cheese are so much a matter of individual taste...seems like cheese-grading would be a pretty tough job.

PMA: Let's see if we can get this straightened out. The grading of cheese is one thing, and the inspection of cheese-making plants is another. Taste is still a third.

ANNOUNCER: Well, let's take grading first.

PMA: Okay. The official grades are U.S. double-A...A...B and so on. Until very recently, the grade marks appeared on what is called the "wheel" --- that's the round shipping box in the case of Cheddar. Naturally, few

PMA:
(continued)   have started putting natural Cheddar and Swiss in consumer-sized packages, bearing the grade stamp.

ANNOUNCER: But isn't it true that I might buy some grade A Cheddar
today which tastes quite a bit different than some of
the same grade from the same company two weeks from now?

PMA: You're sure sticking to that taste business, aren't you?
Well, you're right. But many people can find a
difference in the taste of 93-score butter from week to
week, too. We can't and don't want to standardize
people's taste buds. However, taste does have a bearing
on the grade, just as it does in butter.

ANNOUNCER: I see...it's just that we can't narrow taste down too
much.

PMA: Golly, I don't know how we got into this, but let me try
to end this taste business by saying that as long as the
Cheddar cheese tastes like Cheddar should, then the
grade it will receive depends upon color, texture,
moisture, and such things.

ANNOUNCER: I guess that does end it. Now what about inspection of
cheese?

PMA: A great deal of process cheese is manufactured under
what we call continuous inspection service. This service, again, is voluntary.

ANNOUNCER: That service means that the inspector supervises the
entire operation, doesn't it?

PMA: Yes...it's similar to continous inspection of processed fruits and vegetables. The inspector keeps an eye on raw materials, the finished product, and sanitary conditions of the plant. And since so much processed cheese ends up in small, consumer-sized packages, you can easily check for the familiar shield and the words: "Processed and packed under continuous inspection of the U. S. Department of Agriculture."

ANNOUNCER: And that, as we know, is a guarantee of quality and sanitation. But now, what was it you said about eggs?

PMA: I didn't say anything, yet. But I will say that egg supplies are working toward a seasonal high point, expected in early April.

ANNOUNCER: I have a question, _____. Why does the heaviest egg production come in the spring?

PMA: There are a number of reasons. First, the fall-hatched chicks are getting old enough to start producing. Secondly, last spring's chickens are in their prime. Thirdly, increasing hours of daylight influence production.

ANNOUNCER: Question answered. Are we going to have more eggs this spring than in past years?

PMA: Yes. Or let's say, more eggs will be available. You see, while egg production is only slightly ahead of last year, demands from the Armed Forces, and other countries are less. That means there'll be plenty of

PMA:
(continued)
eggs on the market from now through early summer, at least.

ANNOUNCER: By "plenty" do you mean "too many"?

PMA: Possibly. However, the poultry industry doesn't expect much trouble on that score, so long as folks continue eating lot's of 'em. The industry has set aside March 6 to 15 as a week for encouraging the use of eggs by everyone.

ANNOUNCER: As long as we're urging consumers to buy eggs, let's help 'em buy wisely. Most eggs are graded, aren't they?

PMA: I don't know as you could say "most"...but I believe a majority of eggs are graded. And most eggs are certainly sized. Many states require that eggs be sized and labeled properly.

ANNOUNCER: Let's see...about all I know are large, medium, and pullet eggs.

PMA: Well, there are also extra large eggs, and peewee sizes. Actually, to be scientific about this, th e "sizes" should be referred to as "weights", since the size-class is determined by weighing the egg, rather than measuring its diameter.

ANNOUNCER: But you indicated that the size, or weight has nothing to do with grade.

PMA: No...they're separate items. Eggs are usually graded by the cooperative Federal-State grading services.

PMA:
(continued)   You see, in a medium egg, for example, you can have a
               whole range of grades.

ANNOUNCER: That's logical, now that I think of it. How about
               color, though?

PMA: Color has nothing to do with grade --- I mean the colo:
               of the shell, of course. The U. S. Standards on egg
               grades don't even mention shell color.

ANNOUNCER: Now we have three things that consumers will run into
               in buying eggs --- size, grade, and color. Can you
               coordinate all that somehow?

PMA: First off, I'd prefer to ignore shell color. In some
               places, white eggs are priced higher than browns of
               the same size and grade. But the color of the shell
               has no effect whatsoever on the food value of the egg.
               For that matter, neither does size nor grade.

ANNOUNCER: Hm-m-m. Now I haven't the faintest idea where we
               stand. Just why do they bother sizing and grading
               eggs, then?

PMA: Well, obviously, a dozen eggs weighing 24 ounces ---
               that's large --- is worth more than a dozen weighing
               21 ounces --- mediums. You're getting more egg...but
               the types of vitamins and minerals and so on are the
               same.

ANNOUNCER: Yes...well, then, where do the grades come in?

PMA: From the point of view of the housewife, the grades act
as a guide to buying eggs for different uses. Grades
are based, briefly, on how the egg looks <u>inside</u> the
shell --- size and shape of the yolk, amount of air
space, and presence or absence of blood spots

ANNOUNCER: Then I guess if you wanted your breakfast eggs to look
pretty "sunny side up" you'd get the top grade.

PMA: That's right...the top grade being double-A. Actually,
grade A is fine for home use such as frying, poaching,
or boiling. Then in cooking, where you're going to beat
the egg up beyond recognition anyhow, lesser grades such
as B and C are perfectly all right --- and save you
money, too.

ANNOUNCER: I'm sure glad you got that straightened out...had me
worried for a while.

PMA: Well, it is sort of confusing to balance the factors of
weight and grade --- and sometimes color --- against
each other. So how about getting on to the comparative-
ly simple subject of sugar?

ANNOUNCER: Fine...but I hope it's not so simple that there isn't
any.

PMA: Oh, quite the contrary. It was announced last week that
for the three month periods starting April 1 and July 1,
ration coupons will be worth 10 pounds of sugar, instead
of 5 as we're getting now.

ANNOUNCER: Yes...I figure that at the end of the first nine months
of 1947, we'll have had as much sugar as during the
whole year of 1946.

PMA: However..I'd like to add a litte warning to housewives.
You'll want to watch your sugar supply, because there'll
be no special stamps for sugar for home canning this
year. It's true that we received 25 pounds of sugar for
1946. but you'll recall that 10 pounds of it were issued
especially for the canning season. This year it's
expected we'll get 30 or even 35 pounds per person for
the 12 months, but you'll just have to save home canning
sugar from this amount. And now, _____, it looks as
if we'd better g.. right into the subject of what's
plentiful on the market.

ANNOUNCER: All right. What seems to be leading the parade this
week?

PMA: I don't believe I can put the finger on anything that
might be termed a leading item. Of course, potatoes
and onions might answer that purpose --- they're
certainly plentiful enough.

ANNOUNCER: The only thing is, I guess we've more or less been
taking those two for granted.

PMA: Then I'd like to report the good news that lettuce is
getting more plentiful. You should be able to find
pretty good supplies in most places now.
((NOTE: Because of labor conditions in the
PHILADELPHIA area, these plentifuls may not
be found there. Check locally.))

ANNOUNCER: Good. We could all use a little lettuce to pep up winter meals.

PMA: Meantime, greens of various sorts --- spinach, kale, collards --- continue plentiful throughout the northeas And those two cousins, cabbage and broccoli, are in good supply, too.

ANNOUNCER: How about the root crops?

PMA: Coming up. You'll find beets, carrots, parsnips, and turnips in all markets. Sweet potatoes are available in most markets, too.

ANNOUNCER: ·Guess that brings us to fruit.

PMA: Well, the fruit situation hasn't changed much. There are lots of our northeast apples still around...and of course the citrus fruits continue plentiful. That's it. _____. Thanks for listenin'.

ANNOUNCER: And thanks for talkin', _____. Friends, you've been listening to another session on YOUR FAMILY'S FOOD, with _____ _____, of the Production and Marketing Administration office in _____, and yours truly, _____ _____

# # #

Lightning Source UK Ltd.
Milton Keynes UK
UKHW041152150219
337137UK00013B/1583/P